# GAY & TIRED VOL 2

## TOPHER J GEN

THE SECOND BOOK OF ESSAYS,
THOUGHTS & QUIPS

# Contents

**Introduction**                    9 –11

**Section One:**

Dating & The Gay Scene          14 -49

**Section Two:**

Love: Its Lessons & Aches       51-78

**Section Three:**

Notes on Mental                 79-99

# INTRODUCTION

Hey, I'm internet trash Topher Gen and welcome to my book. First of all, let me express my sincerest gratitude for purchasing Gay & Tired vol 2 (the sequel nobody asked for.) The first volume must have boasted decent enough content for you to repeat the same mistake and buy this; either that or you enjoy wasting money. On the bright side, you've just purchased something that can also double up as a coaster or door stop, so not a total loss – yay for multi-purpose items! Either way, I appreciate it. I mean, you clearly have awful taste in literature but still, thank you.

Before you read any further, I want it noted that this book won't help you lose weight, become smarter, quit smoking, find a boyfriend/girlfriend/magic lamp or stop you from doing that thing where you accidentally bite you tongue - sorry, no refunds.

It will, however, provide an honest insight into all the triggers, catalysts, highs and lows that come at you hard during life. From bad affairs that bleed into lingering heartache, to on-going feuds with friends; from being a victim of the rumour mill, to humiliating moments at parties that make you want to punch a wall in despair. Topics may also include, but are not limited to, career confusion, growing older, curious straight guys I've met at the gym and feeling like a spectator in your own life (living while battling depression.)

We all have those days where we're just a wee confused ball of anger ready to detonate at any given moment. Anger at your boss, anger at your family, anger at your dog because he doesn't opposable thumbs so can't text you back…this book dissects those feelings, while sharing my own battles with them. It basically covers the entire circus show that characterises adulthood for most of us. It won't help you become a better person, but it might make you feel a little less alone (or by comparison less psycho.) After all we're all just world-weary travellers, looking for something or someone to relate to.

There is a surplus of arrogant tit-heads out there roaming the internet, each one preaching their own brand of gospel, telling you how to improve yourself. If only you could miraculously find time to practice yoga forty times a day; or perhaps if you post irksome motivational quotes, you'll suddenly have an influx of confidence.

You know, all that shite.

This book won't lecture you on any of that. It's essentially a glorified coaster for your wine glass. So, if the above is what you're after then I suggest closing this right now. However, if you're looking for insights into life as a member of the LGBTQ+ community, and comments on love, life and heartache, then keep reading. This book documents each little hiccup, break-up, lesson learned and the general zig-zag journey that is adulthood. My aim is to make you feel less alone in your fuck ups - yay for trauma bonding!

There are billions of us. Infinite swarms of people, real people, wrestling with the same issues I face. So, it's my hope someone reads this book and feels a little less crazy, and a little more understood. Failing that, as I said earlier, this book makes a great doorstop.

If you like any of what you read, share your thoughts with me on Twitter. My handle is @TopherJGen and I welcome your comments (unless you don't like it, in which case please hesitate to reach out.) Thank you <3

# DATING
# &
# THE GAY SCENE

## Gays in Common.

Those who live in the UK will tell you that the Scottish scene is so damn small that all gays have, like, one degree of separation. It's essentially just one big Escape Room featuring the ghosts of boys who stopped talking to you to date each other. You literally cannot walk into a gay bar without seeing five guys who have all been inside the same local. It's. That. Damn. Small.

One rainy evening a guy was slinging fairly provocative Snapchats to me – well, not just me. I felt it was one of those 'send to all and see who replies' scenarios. Anyway, I didn't respond. Later that night I sent another guy a message. Its tone was casual, semi-flirty; to be honest it was rather tame for me. Then, moments later, aforementioned guy popped up on Snapchat (clearly his app of choice) and whipped himself into a verbal frenzy, all because I could *"reply to the guy he was with, but not him?"*

Oh, apologies for the late reply to your Snapchat. You see, I'm not 15! Lesson learned here – you never know who is next to the person you're messaging, especially in community this small. Be cautious. After that he stopped speaking to me, yet continues even today to like all my Instagram posts. Honestly, some of the gays in this godforsaken city will really avoid eye contact with you, but for some reason have you listed as a Close Friend on Instagram.

Anyway. That's how small it is. Gays of the world, don't come to Scotland. Unless you want to watch all the boys that ever friendzoned you hang out with someone else you used to date.

**An Evening on Grindr.**

None of us are strangers to lonely nights. You know, the ones that sit uncomfortably in the pit of your stomach like a bad meal. Those achy, late hours that make you contemplate your own mortality. Those nights where your left hand just doesn't cut it and, ideally, you'd rather a ten-inch cock or a munchie box and cuddles. Sadly, life isn't that pretty or perfectly sweet. And loneliness, well, it comes to us all.

If your existence is in any way as mundane as mine, your evenings are probably spent either masturbating until your wrist muscles creak, mindlessly scrolling through Twitter or lying on your bed twitching like a half-crushed spider. All in all, your nights are about as much fun as an MRI scan. It was on one of those nights, I found myself forced to entertain a truly toxic notion.

I am of course referring to the festering skid-mark on the underpants of the digital dating world; an app that's more commonly used as a dick-pic dispensary. It's the gay version of a Pokédex. A creation forged deep in the putrid bowels of the Hades Apple Store. I am of course talking about Grindr. If you have never used Grindr before then I suggest putting this book down; it isn't for people of your calibre, or with your level of self-respect. However, if you decide to keep reading then allow me to illuminate your ignorance by sharing with you a typical Grindr experience.

Grindr has somehow earned itself the mantle of 'dating app', which is a formidable achievement. Especially considering it's not really a conventional dating app at all; it's more a big, online bin full of blank profiles and discount hobgoblins with the occasional penis thrown in to lighten the mood.

You sign in to find that half of its users look like a rejected Gremlin that was fed after midnight, while the other half greet you with unsolicited nudes. It's like logging into a dystopian future where the art of conversation has withered and the once simple *'hello'* has been replaced with an intimate shot of someone's colon.

You don't receive compliments, you receive dick pics and frankly, it's awful. Nothing makes me want to chew off my own arm more than receiving a dick pic from an anonymous stranger. It's the equivalent of a cat bringing you a dead bird as a present.

Yet as heinous and unholy as Grindr is, there's no shortage of characters on it that's for sure. And since it was one of those nights where I wasn't leaving the flat any time soon, I grabbed my phone, logged on and prepared to savour what would surely be the most powerfully underwhelming experience imaginable.

Within 0.7 seconds the first dick pic flopped into my messages. I clicked open and there it was, staring at me, looking like a chubby, throbbing thumb after a hammer smashing.

The culprit wasn't much a better. He was an older man who sported a freshly shaved head and a white, elongated goatee combo that made him look like a cross between an evil wizard and a sick, alternative Santa. Nevertheless, I pressed on, determined to find a potential suiter or at least someone that could stitch together a more coherent sentence than a toddler.

Seven agonising minutes later I realised something: No way in hell was I going to find the type of guy I wanted amongst this cesspit of broken dreams. It soon became clear I needed to lower my standards, because here is the type of guys you typically encountered on Grindr:

### Type One:
### The Unblockables:

That guy who, no matter how many times you block him, keeps coming back like a monster in a movie, or an unpaid bill, or casual racism. He will hound you so incessantly that you'll consider going into Witness Protection just to get away from him. Then, even after that, he'd likely pop up AGAIN. These guys can take dicks but cannot take a hint. The 'conversation' will likely go as follows:

*'Hi.'*
*'You there?'*
*'Looking good babe!'*
*'Wow, you're rude.'*
*'You think you're so hot, but you're actually ugly.'*
*'U there m8?'*
*'Pathetic no wonder ur single'*
*'Hi.'*

Look, you rusted bitch. Let me ladle you a pippin' hot bowl of how it is: I'm a mountain lion and you're a cross-eyed dumpster cat. Take the hint, you aborted queef weasel. I don't want to talk.

## Type Two: The Angry Beige Guy

This one comes in a variety of tribes and is more a personality (or lack of) flaw. His conversation is about as stimulating as a light breeze gently whooshing up your anus, only not as refreshing. You'll seldom make it past the '*how are you*' stage. Then, when his attempts at conversation are rebuffed and met with silence, he will simply reply '*??????????????????*' It's like wishing for sex but being forced to watch paint dry instead. **Note**: There are occasions where these guys evolve from 'beige' to an 'unblockable.'

## The (Overly) Self-Assured Twink

He's barely past the age eighteen milestone, but already he's infused with an arrogant sense of entitlement. His bio will be cold, standoffish and typed all in lowercase letters, because that's what his idle Ariana Grande does. He won't reply as he's younger aka better than you. The full bloom of youth is on his side. Any attempts at conversation will be met with a link to his PayPal, nothing more. He's looking for a daddy you see, but nobody over 25-years-old. FYI, if someone is five/six years older than you, it does not make them your 'daddy', it makes them a second cousin at best.

On the rare occasion he does reply, he'll complain about not having a boyfriend or that he can't afford concert tickets (likely to Ariana.)

## The 'Straight Actin' Guy

A heinous breed of gay. The self-proclaimed 'masc' guys. They don't want anything remotely femme messaging them (an instinctive physiological response to deep-rooted internalised homophobia I bet.) They're into straight acting guys only. They're manly, don't you get it? So macho. Keep your fairy juice away from their testosterone flooded bodies. They're the type of guy that when sending a dick pic, will have a water bottle next to it for perspective. If you send a nude, you'll get nothing but the word 'nice' back (he's too busy grunting whilst watching football or whatever.) If you decide to engage, expect robotic intolerance and haughty judgements on anything feminine about you – cause he's a real man. ROAR!

Too harsh? Perhaps, but that's the typical type of guys we've all met on Grindr.

So, as you can see, there's a variety of human life there, just not anyone you'd want to see naked, or spend the rest of your days with. Or more than an hour of your evening with, come to think about it. The more you're on Grindr, the more a metallic taste of disappointment fills your mouth. It clearly isn't encoded with love, but I suspect most people don't use it for that.

If you're looking for good-boy chivalry and harmless comments, then I don't recommend it. It's all *'Hey baby!'* and *'U want this Dick???'* until you refuse to send a nude and suddenly when you don't respond you get nailed with, *'You're a fucking bitch!'*

Typically, most guys don't handle rejection well, so it escalates fast. My advice? Delete that app as it'll make absolutely no difference to the trajectory of your love life.

## How to Turn Me On

1. Pizza, lots of it.

2. Unattainable guys. Honestly, if you don't want me then I will want you. You could make me feel more worthless than the white stuff that accumulates at the side of your mouth when you're dehydrated, and I'll still follow you into Hades.

3. Someone who can hold a conversation for more than three minutes. Real, stimulating conversation though. Also, make me laugh.

4. A good sense of fashion and style. Be unapologetically you. That's hot. I'm very much of the belief that if you like it, buy it; however, just because you can wear something, doesn't mean you should.

**5.** Booze. I've been single for so long that a few compliments and a double-vodka Coke ought to do it.

## & How to Turn me Off

**1.)** Dirty nails are such a deal breaker for me. Like, you're not putting them near, on or in me. I know it can be because of someone's job, but be conscious enough to think, *'Oh, do my nails look dirty?'* because I don't want to get with someone who looks like they've been burrowing with woodland creatures all day. Clean them.

**2.)** Brunettes: Dying your hair platinum blonde once a year is not a substitute for a personality (although it is a prelude to a break down.) Back up your looks with decent chat.

**3.)** Typing everything in lowercase. I am sorry but this does not make you Ariana Grande. Also, grammar is sexy.

**4.)** No kink shame, but I don't like feet. I dislike even seeing my own, so I most certainly do not want to smell/touch/lick/name/pet yours. So please don't ask.

### The Straight Guy from My Gym.

I'd gone what felt like years without contact from another male. I'd banished Grindr from my phone and boys in bars looked me as though I'd committed some monstrous war crime. My ego was battered while my body had become an unlovable, barren wasteland, desired only by midges and doctors wanting to procure it for medical science.

The lonely days stretched out into weeks, and I spent the nights cuddled up with my insomnia. One time I let my friend borrow underwear, and I swear my Calvin

Klein's were grateful to be touching human genitals that weren't mine.

One bleak Tuesday I decided to focus all this pent-up [sexual] aggression and crippling loneliness into a ridiculously sweaty cardio workout. After I finished, I limped down the stairs with my personal trainer, a muscular woman named Carol whose intimidating physique suggested she could be a stunt double on Game of Thrones for Brienne of Tarth. Carol muttered her usual parting words of praise and I thanked her for listening to me bitch incessantly for forty-five minutes - I try to combine therapy and gym into one. Saves money.

Stealthily I slid into the changing rooms, trying not to gaze out across the sea of flaccid penises and hairy ass-cracks. I started to change out my gym shorts, blending into the lockers like a body-conscious chameleon, when I felt a tap on my shoulder. I paused, hesitant; I was unsure if it was just a ghost or someone else about to make a comment on my debatably 'too short' gym shorts. Then I whipped round to see an attractive guy standing behind me.

He the most pristine baby-blue eyes and was built

like the guys I follow-but-secretly-hate on Instagram. He asked to get into his locker, which was above mine, so I leaped out the way without hesitation. Internally I started to flail and panic, the PTSD from high school gym class threatening to kick in any second. As he started changing, I just stood there looking at him like a terrified animal. After noticing my awkwardness (also the drool coming from my mouth) he started making small talk; as the conversation went on, I started to notice hints of flirtation as well.

He kept talking while I secretly applauded myself for being able to navigate a conversation with a total stranger, in the gym of all places. He asked how my day went, if I had a good work-out, and what my plans were later.

As we spoke, I swear I could see pink, heart-shaped confetti showering down around us; the full pelt of a choir singing a medley of every cheesy love song ever written rang through my head. This was the first hot guy to speak to me using real words, and not keyboard strokes, in a while. A minute or two into exchanging pleasantries and he moves out the way so I can finish changing. As I turned around, I caught him looking and I swear, I SWEAR, he was checking my butt out. For a moment I thought, okay that's cool. I mean, a little sleazy but sure check me out. Hell, objectify me!

I thought that this was it, I was going to be asked out or at least get pumped. Sadly, my dreams were punctured, and my semi-erect penis deflated. A second later he sheepishly switched the topic to what? Oh yes, his girlfriend. As that was his plans for the evening. Whatever mate, I'll see your blank profile floating around Grindr in the not so distant future. I stood silently for a moment before giving him the same look my friends give me when I forget their birthday or buy them shitty Christmas gifts. Listen, I don't need any more crazy, mixed signals. I have my ex for that. The whole affair was about as depressing as eating those tiny sandwiches they serve at funeral receptions.

## Gay Scene Ageism

Over the last two years, getting older has started to scare me. Maybe it's because I still favour nights out over nights in. Maybe it's because I have the constitution of a party girl on 'My Super Sweet 16' and the impulse control of a toddler. Or maybe it's because I've always associated getting older with being written off; with being tossed out by society and not being able to enjoy a healthy, active social life anymore.

The other night whilst out I met an older man. He'd hidden himself in the shadowy corner of the club, swaying awkwardly while nursing his drink, trying to avoid being seen.     I recognized these traits as the hallmarks of social anxiety. It's an affliction I've battled with more times than I care to admit. Never one to see someone standing alone, I wandered over and struck up conversation.

A few minutes into the basic chit-chat and he tells me his age. 'I'm 62', he says sheepishly. He then goes on to express worry that he 'feels too old' to be here. I shrug off this comment and try to soothe his concerns off by assuring him that he has the same right as anyone else to be here. He goes on tell me that he's new to the city and that, when younger, he never had the opportunity to do 'this' (clubbing.) However, a moment later, the conversation stopped mid-sentence when a younger gay (whose face was so smoothed over he resembled a malnourished Ken doll) shot a disparaging glare over towards the man. The look said it all; he was judging this man based purely on his age.

This may be a snap assumption considering all he did was glare wordlessly, but I'm sure a lot of us have seen, or maybe even been victim of, ageist behaviour at some point in a bar or club setting.

I've only ever had a few negative comments made my age, but I'm not going to lie: it really grinds your ass/soul down. I've had nights where I've felt about 8,000-years old after talking to someone who looks young enough to be my offspring. But I've also had periods of extreme burnout before my wisdom teeth had even come in. Therefore, I can't imagine how hard some older men must feel in a scene environment, particularly one that's populated by a horde of half-naked, bouncing twinks.

I've seen it so many times; judging glares from youthful gays at older gay men because they think it's 'weird' or 'creepy' that they're in the same bar. What they fail to realize is that they'll one day be that age. Ageism takes root in denial, in pretending that we'll never get old. But everyone wakes up a day older.

You don't hit 40 and find the urge to visit a bar suddenly eradicated. Nor do you have to retire your social life and commit to a hermit lifestyle. I feel it's somewhat easier for heterosexuals as they have a more options; there's a variety of bars and clubs which are tailored to certain demographics. However, the gay scene – in Scottish cities anyway – lacks in size and thus variety, and because of that we need to be more inclusive.

We are a community composed of all ages, genders and races. We should not be complicit in our further marginalization. The best people I've ever met are the ones who follow the mantra 'age is just a number.' Eighteen or 85, you can go to a gay bar or club and have drinks. You should be able to let loose and dance in a joyous way; you aren't dead yet, so why the hell not?

We need to beat back that 'you're too old' and 'that guy is creepy because he's older' mentality like the medieval dragon it is.

Ageing is an accomplishment. We should feel pride not shame. If I'm still able to have a night out when I'm 60 I'll be doing (metaphoric) cartwheels. Although at this rate, I'll be surprised if I can handle a night out by next June. But what I feel is more important is that we realize what we can learn from each other.

After talking to that older man, I gained perspective and a better understanding of the struggles his generation battled – and he also bought me a drink, so it was a double win!

You can find common ground with anyone, so don't write people off because of their age. We are all a part of the same community.

### Rumour Has It

Age fourteen and I am attending a pretty raucous party. Wearing my token oversized hoodie and armed with two bottles of WKD, I sheepishly slide myself into a corner hoping nobody really notices me. Little did I know that by the end of the next school day I'd be on everybody's radar, as this was the night the first rumour about me was born. Admittedly it was tame in nature compared to the rumours that would outline my social life over the next few years; but to a young, teenage me, this lie felt like being kicked to the ground repeatedly.

Its perpetrator was a girl who, for whatever reason, had a vendetta against me. You know the type, a heinous bitch for no apparent reason; she would run her mouth off to a teacher but wouldn't bust a grape in a fruit fight. She'd moan throughout math class (or any class) because she didn't want to be there. The sort of person that winds up tearing other's down in a pathetic bid to hide her own insecurity. A wee cow, basically.

I don't know why she had such a grudge; maybe it was because I was prettier? Or perhaps it was because the excess puppy fat I was carrying around made my tits look bigger than hers? Honestly, who knows.

Monday morning arrived and I sat in registration class, waiting for the bell to sound and first period to start. Then, from the back of the room, a boy yells a question: *'Did you kiss anyone at that beach party then?'* FYI, I'm from a tiny town with a cluster of beaches that were pretty much undisturbed by the police. People tended to host parties there. Well, most of us anyway. Other less-savoury types tended to congregate at the bus stop on the high street (including the bitch troll that started this rumour about me.)

Following the question there was a chorus of sniggers, noticeable enough for my face to turn an ugly shade of red, but subtle enough for the teacher to turn a blind eye.

'*No!*' I replied, offended.

How could I kiss anyone? For one I was the only gay in a 50 miles radios. And two, I looked like a swollen pre-pubescent manatee. Nobody was coming near this, unless if they had a harpoon.

After my reply I waited for the follow up, and sure as the sun does rise it came. '*That's not what I heard!*' Another wave of laughter washed over the class. In that moment I had a sense of appending doom; they all knew something I didn't – which is ironic considering the thing they knew was about me. Then he blurted it out, with all the aggressive masculinity a boy whose voice was breaking could muster: '*I heard you were caught kissing Eilidh's dog!*'

What was moments ago a mere ripple of laughter, had now swelled into a tsunami of mockery. "Topher Gen. Dog Kisser." Needless to say, there was no weight in the rumour. I didn't kiss the dog; but you know what, if I did, I wouldn't be ashamed because dogs are awesome.

That was the first rumour to go around about me. The subsequent ones that followed in the years to come were a lot rougher and ranged in severity. The usual snooze-worthy *'he's gay, he likes this boy'* themed tales whispered their way around my school corridors for years. Each one more inventive, but equally as tedious, as the last. Yet I survived them. Being lied about and slagged off can be good for you; it thickens the skin and strengthens that backbone. However, years after high school ended, a rumour rooted in lies tore my life apart. It was then I found out just how vicious and destructive they can be.

For the sake of my sanity, and my protection, I won't rehash the story in full detail here. All I'll say is the whole event was dramatized beyond belief. This rumour, and the gossip that followed its conception, raged like wildfire, scorching every aspect of my life, all because some pretentious dick wanted a little bit of attention, so decided reap havoc in my life in order to get it.

Being a victim of a vicious rumour is literal torture of the soul; the very definition of a living Hell. It not only severs you from people, as you don't know who you can trust, but it also cuts your self-esteem and reputation to shreds.

When people lie about you, they're invoking a powerful tool, and the damage that tool inflicts is not easily recovered from. When it happened to me, I lost eighty percent of my friends within the space of two/three weeks. Texts got shorter, I stopped being invited out places. People made it as blatant as possible that I was no longer wanted.

My anxiety grew like a cancerous tumour and my depression got so bad that on some days, I couldn't go out the front door. On nights out I had drinks thrown at me; online, abuse was hurled via anonymous profiles and slanderous words were spat at me in person. It took a tyrannical hold over every aspect of my existence, to the point I was off work for a significant period of time.

Isolation combined with poor mental health is the perfect breeding ground for suicidal thoughts, and the pressure got to the point I tried to take my own life. All because of one twisted individual with deep well of psychological issues decided to make his life seem more interesting but injecting venom into mine.

Why did he do it? Well, why does anyone spread rumours? Maybe they need a narrative to make their mundane life exciting? Perhaps it's a way of conjuring up a collective sense of sympathy? Who knows, but the damage done to the victim of the rumour is incomprehensible because being disliked is not only a is a very specific state, it's also an extremely dangerous one. Especially if the reasons behind it aren't true.

I've had multiple people in my life not like me, and whenever I've approached them to address the matter, asking what the problem was, they'd reply '*I don't know I just don't like you.*' If you have an issue with someone, that's fine; but make sure the reason behind it has some substance. Not just some petty personal vendetta because you heard someone say something that someone else said about the person.

The thing is; rumours die down in time yes, but their essence is always there. And after you're trapped in their web, it can take years to untangle who the person really is beyond their wild reputation. It's harder still for the truth of the matter to emerge when other people don't know what it is - when they only know one-side of the tale. If there's so much of a grain of truth in a story, then people are willing to believe every part of it. No matter how fabricated it sounds or is.

If there's a salient fact that's been managed properly by the culprit of the rumour, the rest of it doesn't matter. Some people are so manipulative they can frame things in such a way that others willingly eat it up. A pre-ordained condition of possibility.

After the rumour I was so irate, hurt and lonely; it felt like a recapitulation of every other rumour ever spread about me. For months I bottled it up. I suffered in silence and never fought back whenever I was given grief about it. How could I? It's human nature to be critical of others and people had already made up their minds.

That's the thing with society, we love a villain. We love a bad guy. We are obsessed with this dichotomy of good verses bad; light against dark. Good witch, bad witch, Glinda and Elphaba. We want two people to embody both sides of the coin, and then we want to destroy them for it.

In the end any rumour, any story, is a lot more ambiguous and complicated than any one party can know. Then, when it dies down, people move onto the next one.

Culture at this point is kind of like a digestive system; we cycle through these ideas of rumours and scandals, both with celebrities and people in our lives, very quickly because we know there's always another one on the horizon. That's all I was; something else to be chewed up and spat out for entertainment.

Eventually I tried to fight back; pointed out the gaping holes and flaws in the story. I made it abundantly clear how the entire arc was flimsy and fictitious. I lost count the amount of times I said, *'that's not true',* but of course nobody listened to my protests, except a few true friends who saw right through it from the beginning. Even though I didn't lie, people were wilfully misunderstanding what I said.

The fact is people take what they want from rumours. Even when they are grilling you for the truth, or your version of it, there's this level of angulation they apply to get what they need. Then when they get what they want they take the pieces they've squirreled away and fit the story together in their own way. By the end of the whole rumour cycle the truth looks like a Picasso painting.

The hardest part of battling a rumour, the thing that rips you open the most, is not being able to control the authorship of your story. Someone else is steering the wheel to make themselves look like the victim, when in reality they are as much a victim as you are a villain - that's to say not at all. Then you're left trying to be, trying to prove, that you're a better person, while people wilfully try harder not to see the good in you. These people see this persona and they continue to stick things to it. It makes them feel better about their own lives and mistakes. It's a suffocating culture.

If you've ever perpetuated a rumour or indulged one that you knew on some level was complete bullshit, then shame on you. You're messing with someone's life

### Left on Read.

What was I thinking? No one knows. Maybe I wasn't even thinking at all. The idea of romance turned my guts into cold cream; it was a profoundly scary concept and one I didn't plan to indulge again. I spent weeks avoiding guys and I'd fine-tuned my personality into that of an ice-blooded long-range military sniper. Then it happened. He popped up on my Instagram and it wasn't long before feelings poured into me like unforgiving black water through the side of a stricken submarine.

We started by going through the inane ritual of liking each other's Instagram photos and Tweets - it's essentially a warm-up before you start talking, isn't it? Conversation lubrication. A few days later I slid into his DMs and asked if he wanted to go for a coffee this week. He replied quickly, *'I'd love that!'* And just like that, my sworn oath to avoid love was broken, lasting a total of eight minutes.

The first date went well, much to my and everyone sitting around us surprise. When we got to the cautionary pre-goodbye stage my nerves started to kick in; but before I had a chance to say/do something stupid, he asked if I wanted to go out again – I of course said yes (actually think I sort of screamed it, but anyway.)

Date number two was also a roaring success. I'd let him choose the restaurant and me being the glimmering embodiment of a gentleman, offered to pay for the meal too. Later that evening we had our first kiss. It was in the split-second moment that followed I knew I was falling too fast, too hard. Looking back, if that ever happens again, I'll take it as a sign to back up a bit; but hindsight is always 20/20.

Within a fortnight we'd reached our fifth date. And even after seeing me drunk dance he remained interested (imagine R2D2 zipping across the dance floor looking like a fucking spiked trash can, it's kind of like that.)

It's amazing what a cute guy being enamoured with you can do for your mental health. You no-longer feel the relentless pinch of loneliness and the days don't seem as overcast. It felt amazing; this guy popped up out of nowhere and breezed into my life like a breath fresh air. He made me feel so special in such a short space of time that for the briefest, and most blissful, of periods I didn't think about how fast we were going. Until, whilst riding out a hangover on a sticky Saturday afternoon, we came to a jittering halt.

It was the height of summer, and it was one of the four days a year where Scotland is gifted blazing heat. Yet we spent the day in bed; me rolling hard on antihistamines to combat my life-ruining hay fever, whilst he suffered through a gloomy come-down.

He'd came straight from the party he'd attended the night before and crawled into my bed comfortably. I didn't mind that he hadn't showered since yesterday morning, or that he had an anxious grin fritzing across his face like an android gone wrong; or that his pupils were so dilated it made him look possessed Furby. I was just happy to be around him. Later that evening, after we'd recovered enough and regained full control of our bodies, we ended up sleeping together – our first time. No awkwardness, no regrets; it felt nothing short of right. We then clambered out of bed, showered, then I made us dinner. Shortly after he left mine via my wardrobe borrowing a hoody, before heading off to work. Then he vanished off the face of the earth. Totally kidding, but that was the last time I saw him.

**Note**: I have since seen him and had to fight the urge to punch him in the oesophagus.

Seven days drudgingly passed, and I'd reached a stage of disappointment that I considered the sexual equivalent of an annulment. When I phoned, he screened my calls; if he uploaded something, I'd like it, yet he stopped acknowledging my posts. Eventually I reached the point of psychosis where you message multiple times, despite always being left on read.

*'It's been a week and he hasn't text me back!'* I screamed at my friend so loudly that half the country got earache. *'He'd better be sick! Like, so sick someone writes a YA novel about him. That's the only excuse I'm accepting!'* What was so terrible about me that it made him lose interest?

Most people would simply pick up the massive 'left on read' hint and call it a day, but I needed an explanation. How hard is it to conjure up the strength to be honest? Some guys are just cowards. Another week ticked by and still I heard nothing, so naturally I started blaming myself. My confidence begun to dwindle in his absence. I was filled with a sense of panic: was I so bad in bed that guys considered keeping their trainers on just so they can make a swift exit after it? Is sleeping with me like being dicked by disappointment itself?

Soon I reverted to my familiar state of not feeling good enough. He obviously didn't want me, and as if that wasn't bad enough, he wouldn't even give me a reason.

It's amazing how we hand over power to guys we like, isn't it? We give them the ability to flatten our egos and crush our hearts until nothing remains but useless dust. One negative opinion or terrible treatment from someone can silence all the praise given to you by others; forcing you to reject all the self-love you've built up. You give someone your time and they can make you feel as though you are worth jack squat to them; that you're nothing more than a speck of dust in the universe; a tiny drop of water in a bathtub. A tile in a complex mosaic. A solitary, insignificant pixel on an immense and terrifying LCD screen. A few words, or in this case a lack of words, and suddenly my sense of worth dropped so I low I just felt like giving up on romance AGAIN.

Eventually, 13 days later, while I was channelling all my anger into a 10k on a treadmill at 6:30am, he sent me a paragraph-long explanation that featured the phrase, and I shit you not, '*it's not you, it's me.*'

YOU ARE DAMN RIGHT IT'S YOU!

The moment I read that line I had to fight the urge to throw a bike through his window.

The rest of the message stated that he wasn't ready for a relationship; that's he's battling his own demons and right now he can't commit to anything tangible. It went on to say that I'm a great guy, but I should be with someone who mirrors what I want in a relationship.

The thing is, I'm a decent person. And while I appreciated the honesty, I couldn't help but harbour slight resentment that he didn't bother to explain, even briefly, any of this before.

Despite being pissed off, humiliated and heartbroken over his radio silence, I still extended a warm, helping hand to him in my reply – which was rebuffed, by the way (yup, left on read, again.)

I wasn't sure if his reasons were factual and rooted in truth, or if they were put together to try and reduce the sting that follows being ghosted after you shag someone. I wasn't sure how any of this happened to be honest, but one thing I did know: I now trusted guys to consider my feelings as much as I trust people to respect upholstered seating on public transport.    In the time it took for me to grow a decent amount of facial hair, I'd fallen-for-then-lost someone. I mean, it wasn't a record for me, I once managed to scare a guy away within 24 hours (we did it, ladies) but this was a close second. I kept expecting a rosette to be sent via the post for being the most undateable guy in the Northern Hemisphere yet, much like his reply, it never came.

**Rating**: I am going to lock myself in a hermetically sealed environment and avoid all contact with anything that has, or is, a penis.

# LOVE, LESSONS & ACHES

## Falling for a Friend.

Falling for a friend is a familiar heartache that so many of us have shared. Every moment in each other's company can be thick with confusion; you don't know if you'll feel one thing, or another. It can cause tension that is neither sexy or sustainable and break your heart with such finality you're uncertain if either of you will ever be able to fix it.

As hard as it is, when it's over you have to quietly face facts and reconcile with the heartache of losing not one, but two relationships: The past friendship that you can never return to, and the future romantic one created in your head. It can leave you standing in a temporary space, seeking a way out, but desperate to stay. For me, falling for a friend was a lesson in honesty; one that teaches the importance of being upfront as, no matter how close you are, you risk losing more by saying nothing.

I never picked my crushes wisely; you could even say that I've always had a penchant for the wrong type of guy. Ones that were hot, but never fully available; those boys that came armed with six pack abs, but also an uncertainty about what they wanted. Some had such a strong lack of empathy it bordered on sociopathic, and others left me feeling as though I looked like Dobby the House Elf after any date we went on.

After each bad break-up I would resign myself to life of cheap wine, takeout and Netflix binges. I'd mutter statements like *'I am going to die alone'* with a tragicomic self-awareness. For the most part I was okay with that. It just seemed the way it was. Then one day it changed, I met someone new. And while we started as friends and ended in the same way, there was a period in the middle where I was convinced we not only would be more, but we also should be.

He came into my life with ease, and the comfort we felt around each other was instantaneous. If I were being poetic, I'd say that I felt like Peter Pan having his shadow sewn back on by Wendy; as if he helped reattach an essential piece of me. There were no seizing silences, or shuttered conversations. It was chemistry from the get-go. During those first weeks together, I revelled in his attention like a kid who got the lead in a school show. I felt like I was now playing on a levelled field, one that was different from the downward slope I was used to living on. There were days when I got up first, and days when he did. We took turns making tea and lost hours to relaxed silences over movies. Days together in bed blanketed by a knowledge that words weren't required – just each other's company. But our time together would soon offer nothing but a blurring of lines.

The few times we kissed I felt the electricity hang in the air. Shortly after, all admirable boundaries were broken down and we started sleeping together. Then the enviable creeped up and I found myself losing my breath whenever he smiled. Back then I thought I could represent something to him; something understanding, beautiful. I was an adult, I was grounded, I was falling in love and I thought he felt the same; but slowly it all started to unravel.

The more we were together, the more our feelings evolved separately. I tried to outline and define our time as something beyond the borders of friendship, but for him it unfolded differently. There would be no dates, only the kind of loving but overly careful nights together, with our space for comfort slowly being replaced by a distance measured in unsaid truths.

I started borrowing time from other friendships and investing it in him. A side-effect of this was he soon became my entire world – while I merely remained a small part of his. It was hard, in that moment, to summon would it could be and accept what it wasn't. So, I became clingier, and he grew more distant. Our friendship remained the same but was now infused with an implicit tension. Eventually we stopped sleeping together, then we stopped kissing and soon we were separated by more than just pieces of clothing.

One night the pressure swelled and under the weight of uncertainty I buckled, telling him through drunk, teary eyes how I felt. For a moment there was silence; I sat waiting with my head arched down toward my legs, somewhere between a panic attack and grieving. After what felt like a lifetime, he confirmed with a shaky totality that my feelings were not reciprocated. The illusion of connection had been severed and I found myself silently wishing for my room to catch fire so I could get out of this situation.

It was too late though, by this point I was already chemically changed. The independence I once knew had been replaced with a mourning that could only be soothed by his constant company. Rather than admit how crushed I felt, I wiped my eyes and said, *'that's fine as long we can still be friends.'* He smiled and agreed.

I was determined to make peace with this fact. To make the friendship work. In a desperate bid to get over him, I'd snatch any attention offered up to me. I knew these flings were fleeting; they were as false as they were finite. But like all meaningless sex, it offered the temporary remedy of forgetting; and I figured if I could forget long enough, one day I'd wake up over it – who hasn't shared that thought process?

The weeks limped by and the friendship slowly started to splinter. Whenever he introduced me to or mentioned another guy, I was infected with a venomous rage. When he didn't reply to my message or conjured up flimsy excuses to get out of plans, I'd sit in my bedroom, filled with desperate, sickened longing. I was so convinced of the wrongness of our separation that I couldn't see how detrimental it was becoming to both my mental and physical health – still, I couldn't let him go.

When I found out he'd been sleeping with other guys I was consumed with such fury that had I been a super villain, I'd have sought global destruction immediately. I'd went from having the most idyllic time with him, to resenting him for numerous reasons that lacked both logic and fairness. Eventually I realised that condemning him for hurting me was unjust.

My feelings had remained buried deep. I never articulated how I felt apart from that one evening, but my hush was born from a fear of losing him altogether. This silence was the deadly kind as in the end, it all proved too much for both parties. The fallout was explosive and prolonged; it embedded a hurt so potent that for a while I thought that, much like a war-torn landscape, I'd never be able heal or grow again. Lying about how I felt was not only detrimental to my sense of self, but it also derailed a great friendship.

For weeks after I scavenged the wreckage; looking out at scraps of regrets and parts of truths I never said, trying to find some way to piece us back together.

All the while knowing this was a disaster that could have been avoided had I only listened to my needs.

I realise now with a power and presence that was lost to me at the time that there were faults on both sides. Had we both been completely honest, and had I thought with my head and not that thing in my chest, we could have reached a peaceful resolution quicker. Sometimes you have to surrender to the truth; bow down and accept that time apart may not be what you want but is what you need.

Now we talk, carefully. Each word is said with precision, but it's a something. It took months of stops and starts, of try and try again; of awkward run-ins at parties and pubs, with a side-serving of fights and apologies. Eventually we have got to a place where I feel we could again be friends. Now we have found a ground that perhaps, if we try hard enough, we'll be able to grow a new friendship from.

**Delicate.**

*"I don't think I'll ever really get over him."* That's the refrain I muttered to anyone who would listen after he left my life the first time. I could hardly count the amount of nights I spent crying over him; the number of days his absence pushed me to the edge of unstable. Living with the heartache of a future without him on the horizon.

I spent months limping toward a fresh start, all the while trying to push him out my system the way addicts do drugs. I wrote countless essays about it, about us, each one triggered by a different moment or memory: the day I found his orange toothbrush in my bathroom; the night I figured out he'd cheated by smelling someone else's cologne off him; and even the moment, as inevitable as it was, I realised he wasn't built to love me the same way I did him.

Like all who have suffered heartache, I felt trapped and alone on an island; marooned there as punishment because I fell for the wrong guy. I'd again failed to adapt myself to romantic love, and now I had to wait to be rescued, never realising that I had to save myself – which, in the end, I did. Somehow, I got through it. I got over it, I got over him. Until a two-years later when he crept back into my life.

His arrival was one I welcomed without a modicum of hesitation, and under the guise of friendship we started spending time together. First it was overly careful check-ins that follow a long-term separation; followed by silently tense social meets for coffee or a walk about town. Then time announced it was safe to be around each other, so down dropped our guards and in ushered evenings of dinner dates and drinks. Sometimes spending three, even four, nights a week together.

I was firm in my belief that I could navigate a friendship. For one we'd both grown emotionally; our conversation was no longer laced with an awkwardness, nor was there any worry one of us would say something wrong and trigger a fight. Where resentment once stood there was now forgiveness. All bad blood had been washed away.

It had been nearly three months of us being friends and still I hadn't succumbed to even a tinge of romantic feelings. It seemed to be playing out well. Then one day, after losing ourselves in conversation, I caught a snippet of who he used to be – of who we used to be. That moment announced itself loudly and hit hard, then old flames started to reignite.

After that split-second change everything immediately felt different. The atmosphere had a current of possibility surging through it; now he looked at me with a familiar fondness, and I allowed myself to do the same. Before I knew it, the flirtation began and then rapidly started to spin out of control. Later that week he'd came to my flat and the chemistry continued to grow. I knew at my core this wasn't harmless anymore, yet we let our emotions conquer us. Want (stubborn, unyielding, relentless want) beat back logic, bridging the gap between us. Eventually he said he needed to leave, and the sinking feeling that had routinely outlined our previous time together returned. So, I pulled him in for a hug, and we both held each other tightly.

I felt his breath on my neck, while our chests pounded against each other. Hearts in cages screaming to be free. The air was thick was anticipation, with right and wrong; we both knew what we wanted yet I pulled away, delivering only a kiss on the cheek. As I walked him to the door, he held one of my hands, then again leaned in and hugged me. He said goodbye and with his hallmark grin left the flat saying he'd message me later.

It is impossible, in moments like that, not to access old feelings; you're reminded how valuable you were to each other. That night I lay in my bed, thinking of the first time we met on the chilly April day. All our memories came back in technicolour, full of odd, quiet details, leading up to the first time I told him '*I love you.*' Lying there I realised how delicate I was when it came to him; I hadn't so much got over my feelings, but rather I'd shipped them far away, somewhere they could no longer do any damage. Now, they'd found me again.

Over the next few days there were brief spaces between his replies. With every message I felt choppy and unseen, like an old TV set that needed the sharpness adjusted. I didn't know what was going on with us; all I could see was the blurred shape of someone I used to love once again coming into focus.

When old feelings come back, you suffer a time lapse interruption of your past. The bad moments remain in the shadows and you focus solely on the good times, which are perfectly calibrated to make you think that this could again be together. That's what was happening. All the hurt, anguish, mistakes and fights that derailed us before no longer posed a threat. But one fact demanded to be heard: I knew we wouldn't work.

Chemistry had a different idea, and inevitably we once again ended up in my room; the history of a few days before threatening to repeat itself. From my side he came and wrapped his arms around me, burying his face in the thick cotton of my t-shirt. Somehow, we were again holding each other too tightly. In those few seconds I tried to understand if I could love him once more, if we'd be able to build a life together this time. Could we now learn from the mistakes that defined our past and stand by each other in way that was foreign to us before?

I hoped against hope that I would be struck by a sign that I should let this happen. Then, like magnets, our lips reflectively pulled toward each other's, my hands bringing him closer but wanting to push us apart.

Suddenly it felt like the whole universe was watching to see what would happen next...but we all know what did. We kissed.

Afterwards I landed a soft kiss on his cheek, saying without prompt, '*I love you.*' He waited a moment before burying his face into my T-shirt once again, replying only, '*I know.*'

Later that night I tried to fend off intrusive thoughts: Is he flirting with someone else? Is he kissing someone else? He sabotaged us last time by cheating, what's to say he won't do it again? I don't have ownership over his actions, I can't control what he does.

I refused to cave under the weight of my growing anxiety, so instead I messaged him saying I hope he has a good time with his friends, and that we can do a movie night soon. Later he replied saying '*thank you*', ignoring without shame the second part of my text.

'*I'm think I'm still in love with him*' I moan to my friend, while we're drinking cheap wine and catching up, wondering how I've turned another single summer into a rollercoaster of overlapping emotions. With a blank expression he suggested wordlessly that I should know better. '*He's playing you*' was all he said.

I decided shortly after that it wouldn't [couldn't] go any further. As much as I loved him, I must respect that he has a new life, and that I am someone else now; we can't and don't work. I needed to honour that fact, even if that thing in my chest protested it.

Realising nothing could come of this, of us, had its minuses and pluses. I started to regain a sense of freedom that allowed me to [slowly] repair parts of myself. With each passing day I felt healthier, brighter and shackle free. As for the minuses, I no longer had an excuse to act like an asshole or parade my feelings around, letting them take priority over anyone else's. I also had to endure the drawn-out agony of once again kicking a habit and stitching up an old wound. The thing about sobriety – much like quitting him – is to know when it's time to leave the proverbial party; knowing where to draw the line and knowing when to say, 'I've had enough.'

This moment in my history has forced me to ask myself what I want from love; and while right now the narrative playing out in my head is one where him and I are together, I know I need to be with someone who will make me feel secure, safe and at home. Not just aroused, jealous and infatuated – because really, that isn't sustainable. I need to accept with totality that friends are all we can ever be. The magic trick here is to not land myself in a situation where lines could be blurred; the lesson here is learning to separate want from reality. Just because the image I have of him - of us – plays out like a cinematic daydream in my head, does not mean it would unfold like that. You may find yourself lost in the idea of someone, but it doesn't mean that's who they are.

That's all I ever did/do with him; I took the snippets I wanted to see and pieced together this perfect picture, ignoring all the bad parts.

All I did here was create another pretty concept of us, of what 'could happen.' Something that was as misleading as his temporary affection; as unrealistic as it was heart-breaking. An idea that was too delicate to ever hold itself together.    Both back then, and now.

## The Other Guy.

Infidelity is not something I am particularly moralistic about anymore. I don't condone cheating, but I'm not so naive as to think all relationships sail smoothly or that mistakes don't happen. I'm also wise to the temptations this 'upgrade' society we live in offers us.

I think at some point most of us have been involved in a situation where we have felt an inappropriate, and often intense, attraction to someone. It could be something as trivial as sudden arousal from stumbling upon nudes online; it could be engaging in flirty behaviour, short and brief, with someone who isn't your partner – or it could be more.

Many of us have fallen prey to the wild aphrodisiac that is infidelity; the seductive lure of doing something you know is wrong. Where the temptation to be with someone else, even just once, has you fixated.

I have been to all corners of the love triangle – none of which fill me with a sense of pride. I've been the one who cheated, although admittedly it was back in high school so I'm not sure if it really counts. I was still half-in the closet at that point, telling my peers I was bisexual because, honestly, it made life a tiny bit easier. The guys in my year tended to relent slightly with the bullying when they believed there was still a modicum of chance that I liked vagina.

In order to keep up this not-so-convincing charade I started dating a girl in my year, (Lynsey, if you're reading this, you were a fabulous beard, honey, thank you) and while we were 'together' we watched seasons of Charmed and occasionally held hands during some episodes. That was about as dedicated to the role as I got.

During our brief tryst, I started fooling around with a boy a couple of years above me. I thought I was being careful, covering up our clandestine affair and romantic beach hook-ups with solid excuses as to my whereabouts but apparently, I wasn't as sleekit as I thought.

After waddling back from a party, drunk off my ass, I stupidly put this boy's initials in my MSN name, decorating them with love hearts hung on each side. In my defence it was probably around midnight, so I just assumed my 'girlfriend' would be in bed. Which she was. However, her friends weren't and so I was exposed as a floozy cheat. Oh, don't judge me; I was about 14 years old at the time, and I felt really bad about it afterwards – although I'm not sure if I felt bad about the cheating or bad that I got caught.

I've also been the one cheated on. Which, and you'll know this if it's happened to you, fucking sucks donkey dick. It's not unlike being knocked to the ground, over and over, while an audience shrieks and applauds. That said, I've tortured him enough in the public forum, so I'll not rehash that story here. Most recently though I've also been the 'other guy' - the one who he would cheat on his boyfriend with; the homewrecker as we're often branded.

The whole situation threatened nothing but torment, trouble and tears yet I allowed myself to dive in willing. Why? Because I fell for the guy, duh. Yet as exciting as being with him was, time would soon show me that there's also an isolating element that comes from being 'the other guy'. For every stolen kiss and secret touch, there was a charge of guilt - the cost of getting what you want at someone else's expense. Having previously been in love with the guy I allowed myself to get swept away quickly; and in a matter of weeks, if not days, I was head over heels again. It was a dark period of my life and when it started up it broke up the tedium of living day-to-day lifelessly.

Situations like this can tear down the monotony of singledom. They can burst through that stale blockade which refuses to let any fresh excitement into your life. I'm not conjuring up flimsy excuses, all I'm saying is I'd spent months in a depressed haze, genuinely feeling as though I had nothing to live for. Then he came along, and suddenly I was in love. What seemed to be an endless grey existence now had flickers of colour injected into it; the feeling of not being good enough for anyone, or anything, was soon replaced with sense of being complete. My life seemed to accelerate from pointless, to full of possibility.

It wasn't a fling born from drunken horniness, or because I was bored, and he was there. I truly had feelings for the guy; and even though at the time it felt all too worth it, it would soon cost me a set of morals I'd clung to my whole adult life. Love makes you selfish. Love makes you cruel. Love makes you blind.

When this guy came back into my life unannounced, we started out as friends. To say I carried a torch for him previously would be a colossal understatement, because the truth is, I used to be in love with him. It was effortless to fall back into that.

After a week together it was as though we'd never been apart. And even though there was an immediate resurrection of physical attraction, it was the web of complicated emotions I found myself got caught up in.

It started out with a flurry of flirtish digs; inside jokes that were coined and reserved only for us. Slowly they lead to goodbye hugs that lasted a few seconds too long but somehow never feel long enough. Then it started to progress, and before I knew it, we were lying beside each other in my bed.

Even before we ended up in that moment, there were a significant number of smaller events that, in my opinion, constituted as cheating. Dinners together, holding hands, near-kisses and showing each other nudes.

Whenever he'd go to leave, I felt as if some irreplaceable part was being torn from me. He'd get moody if I spoke to other guys, I got mad when he checked someone else out or spoke about his boyfriend. From the get-go there were clear indicators that this could never be 'just friendship.' Yet, defiantly, I ignored them all.

Although nothing had [yet] happened, every fibre of my being knew what we both wanted. It screamed silently inside us, while our bodies remained frozen. Every time we were together, I got a kind of endorphin dump; a surge of dopamine followed by a wave of serotonin. I had all these chemicals flooding my brain because of this new romance with somebody that, for the longest time, I wanted to be with. Eventually it reached boiling point and we kissed while lying there together on my bed.

To this day I am unsure how I even landed myself in the situation. One minute we barely spoke passing each other in the street; the next we were talking daily and seeing each other a couple times a week. The whole time this was playing out I asked myself two questions 1) What outcome was he hoping for? 2) If we were together, could I ever truly trust him?

It's an old cliché but also a time proven temptress; you want what you can't have. That's what this new, or rather rekindled, connection was. A taboo affair with a fresh element of possibility and excitement injected into it. The whole time we were together we had to practice all the exercises of subterfuge. We had to mask what this really was as friendship and keep our feelings hidden; but rather than shy away from the public eye, we became cocky with it.

I'm not sure who we were trying to convince more; ourselves, the world or his partner. I guess I figured that if we painted an innocent image of our relationship then there'd be absolutely no reason for anyone to suspect otherwise. I guess I hoped I'd believe that myself, that I wasn't doing anything wrong.

Yet I was doing something wrong; I knew I was. Does that make a cunt? Yes. Does it make me selfish? Absolutely. Does it make me a bad person? No, not exclusively, but before I had a chance to stop all my former feelings had flooded back. I was again in love with him; irreparably, stupidly, willing. I tried to kid myself this would be worth it, that it was going somewhere; but his situation had only ever promised one outcome from the start, and eventually it caught up with us.

Uplifting feelings turned into a relentless pressure; admiration morphed into addiction; and when I was denied what I needed (to see him) it led to severe mood drops. Just like all things that get you high, he also promised to bring me down, and that's what was happening now: the cold crash to reality.

Eventually the ecstasy of being with him gave way to a bombardment of guilt and hopelessness. What was the point of holding his hand? Of secret moments and stolen kisses? Him saying we'd be together if he wasn't with his partner soon held no sway over me. What was the point of him, of us, if it wasn't permanent? I knew at the end of the night he'd walk out my door and back into the arms of someone else. One night I flew into a fit of jealous rage after I caught him trying to kiss a random guy at a party we were at. In that moment I realised I wasn't the 'other guy' but simply 'another guy.' He apologised; he said he just wasn't used to the attention, so he got swept up in it. I found that hard to believe, considering all I did with shower him with it. Shortly after that incident he left the party because he didn't want to 'upset me.' A few hours later he was back at mine, saying he loved me. The spark I felt whenever we were together was now a constant, dull ache that sat in the pit of my stomach. Heartbreak, deceit, emotional carnage: that was all that awaited us if we continued down this road.

The thrill of a clandestine affair vanished, and in its place was a cruel truth. He was never mine. Even though there had been tangible feelings, they were ones I knew he would never reciprocate, at least not fully. I'd only ever get 85% from him.

This wasn't just an affair to me; it was a gateway to a potential relationship. It was a chance to conquer what we never could before - but you can't build new love on a foundation of betrayal and skewed morals.

After I showed a girlfriend a draft of this essay, she said to me quite candidly, and rightfully, *'How can you trust someone who has already cheated? How could you do that to another person?* 'Shitty situations have the magic to cast a glamour over themselves; they have a way of making you see what you want to see rather than ugly, cruel reality. A relationship can't bloom from stolen kisses; just as me being in love wasn't a justification for taking what I want at the expense of someone else's happiness. There was no future for us from the start. I left this situation worse off than I started: Guilty, stripped of my morals, and alone.

## He's All Yours.

I feel a lot of us have been in that precarious situation where you're the half that loves that bit harder. A place where your value as a person becomes intertwined with how much the person you've fallen for loves you back.

I've been there; I've held people in such high regard that, at times, I honestly couldn't believe they'd show me a slither of attention, let alone date me. This is a treacherous slope to land on because a side-effect of giving someone this power over you is you start to feel less special when you are on your own.

When it was me, I felt everything I had was a surface reflection of his greatness, of his looks, his love. Guy's would stare at him, flirt with him online; they'd genuinely swoon over his entire sense of being. So, when I thought I 'had' him (as much as you can ever truly have anybody) it created an illusion that I was happy, that I was worth something. I felt better as a person because I was with him. But that blind devotion didn't alter the fact our relationship was held together by the most tenuis of gossamer strings.

My love continued to evolve while his remained stationary, and that became suffocating and toxic for both of us. I wanted him too much, I loved him too much. And when I didn't get back what I gave out, I sat questioning what was wrong with me – and if he even he cared at all.

Whenever he'd go on a night out, I felt physically sick. I knew he was in a place where other people could look at him, where other people could potentially take him from me. That kind of obsessive behaviour didn't just stem from paranoia; on some level I knew he wasn't as in love with me as I was with him. The fear that his eyes, and hands, would wander looped in my head.

Eventually I started to think *'well, I don't blame him if he did.'* How toxic is that? I constantly gave him my all, and survived on scraps of affection he gave when, and if, it suited him. Soon my self-worth plummeted to such a level that I genuinely believed I was the problem, and that him looking at other guys was justified.

When you're more attached than him, you become the more vulnerable person in a relationship; you start to not feel safe. When that happened to me, I started to act out.

Guys would flirt with him at parties, then I'd wind up yelling. I got into arguments with friends whenever they told me *'you need to grow up and walk away.'* I even started fights with him because, when he hurt me, it meant he'd at least come over and say sorry; he'd show me some form of affection. All this behaviour was because it was no longer love, but infatuation.

When it gets to that stage you hold on for dear fucking life. You fight to keep the sense of worth that he gives you. So, I rode that horse until I got bucked off. Then, when the inevitable came knocking and he ended it, I did whatever I could to get him to come back. It never worked, and in the end all that was left of us was pathos and unbuildable bridges. Love like that is finite; it can't survive.

**Like the Movies.**

As I write this, I'm still glamorizing your behaviour; I tell myself that you're simply misunderstood, and that you are just as sad, scared, and lonely as the rest of us. I conjure up excuses for the liberties I let you take with me; justifying how you keep me on retainer, employing me only to fill the emotional blanks someone else couldn't. Always asking me to act out the parts others refuse. I idealise you; I romanticize us.

I pretend I'm not a fool for being convinced that this on-and-off ambiguous relationship, that has spanned two years, was normal. I tell myself I'm not an idiot for believing you'd eventually be with me, and that one day we could steer onto our own path – but I am a fool. I am; because our trajectory was always tragedy. I was hopelessly in love, and you were just hopeless enough. I try to remind myself that this isn't the movies; that the space between us cannot be filled with wishes, hope and glamour. In this love we don't have equal parts, and our scenes together always end in the same way. No, this isn't the movies. This is real life. And in real life actions have consequences, just as desires often go unmet. This constant stream of heartache, hurt and confusion is not for entertainment, but rather an on-going symptom of our time together.

With each passing day every kiss, touch and compliment has become less sincere and more manipulative. I know there is no enlightenment to be gained from letting you dictate my emotions, yet I surrender my reign to you, hopeful for a happy ever after. And every time I believe you'll finally give me that, you stutter over your lines in the following scene.

You make lights in my head buzz then dim; you look at me in a way I want to last forever, but afterwards it never lingers. You ignore me for days on end and reply to when it suits; you have me where you want me. So, this, I've decided to believe, is the best part you've ever played. You're the starring role in my life.

Perhaps there was never a chain of continuity between the person and persona; between who you are and who I tried to script you to be. Maybe they've always existed as separate entities; the one I created versus the reality – the boy in the movies doesn't match the boy in real life. Our love is a constant rehearsal of guilt.

Instead, I'm praying for the relief of an immediate dismissal; for you to tell me you don't want me in your life, so I'd have no other choice but to go. I am begging you to tell me to leave, to end this scene between us – because I don't think I'm strong enough to walk away from you, again.

# NOTES
# ON
# MENTAL

## You, Yourself & Your Mental Health.

I have a few questions for you. Okay, first up. How many of us have suffered some sort of public rupture? Maybe it was a meltdown in front of people at a party, or you entered a screaming match on a night out? Perhaps you were a victim to the corrosive effect of gossip, or you saw an ex kiss somebody else and contemplated burning the building down?

It may even be one those days where a seemingly insignificant moment causes you to snap, catapulting your sanity to into orbit which results in a spectacular emotional collapse. You know, the sort of outburst that sees onlookers slowly edge towards the door.

Okay, next question: How many times do you hear the word 'crazy' used to describe someone's behaviour/actions in everyday vocabulary? Not even just that word specifically, it could also be something like mental, batshit, psycho, loco...honestly any of its synonyms.

Right, third question - and pay attention because there's a pop quiz at the end of the book (there isn't really.) How many times do we use those words to label someone who is demonstrating the behaviours in question one? *'Girl, she's lost it.' 'What the fuck is he doing?ca-raaaazy gay.* 'I'm willing to bet the answer to all three is a lot of us.

The reason I asked those questions is because lately I've became acutely aware of not only my mental health and the way my friends perceive it, but also the cultural attitude society has toward it. More specifically the thing I've noticed is that even though we talk about it, very few people truly understand it.

When you hear the term 'poor mental health' what does it mean to you? For some it's seen little more than a flimsy excuse to justify someone else's shitty behaviour. For others, it's a signal to turn away, or not text back, rather than ask what's wrong. But for those who suffer from it, particularly depression, it's a daily affliction that leaves you trapped in a constant low mood, severely impairing your ability to handle situations or approach them rationally.

We all know what mental health means, but a lot of people use it as a blanket term. Some never apply the correct individual labels, but rather say someone has 'mental health issues.' They throw everyone into the same category. As a result, the cultural stereotype a lot of people hold is one that sees us all strapped to a gurney, drooling, swearing at a lamp for stealing our sweets.

This attitude toward mental health sees some people use words associated with it in a negative context. Occasionally they are even weaponized and used against sufferers. Don't believe me? Ask yourself this: how many times have you heard whispery bitches saying X, Y and Z about someone because they were going through a bad period of mental health?

So, I want to take some time to talk about mental health, our attitudes toward it, and how much we really know about the carnage it causes.

## The C-Word

It's 2019 and I feel society has developed what I like to call a benevolent neglect toward mental health issues. People are aware that it's a growing issue, but don't grasp the severity of it – and one of the most frustrating results of this neglect is the idea that people should recover quicker than they do.

The thing with mental health is no-one ever recovers on a timeline that's convenient for others, so eventually people get bored of hearing the pleas of a 'sad' person. At first you get all the *'poor baby!'* sympathetic comments, but then after a while people shift towards an attitude of indifference. Their refrain goes from deep concern to blasé mutterings of, *'oh, that sucks.'* They've heard it before, so they don't want to hear it again; which is fair enough because at the end of the day other people can only help you so much, right? No.

While I believe you've got to take steps to get yourself better, there's no excuse for others to be a dick about it. There's nothing more isolating than feeling abandoned or a burden to those you've reached out to,

When the support around you begins to fracture and disappear, you're stuck with your hurt alone. And since your pain is not a physical one with tell-tale symptoms, people tend to forget about it or turn a blind eye. Or worse they start judging you for it behind your back, using words such as crazy, mental and so on. What do you do then? Personally, I shut off. I repress everything and turn into a glacier. Sometimes I contemplate finding a cave and moving into it.

There have been times where I've not had the help I needed. My support networked collapsed and it resulted in a nuclear meltdown in front of a not-so-understanding crowd. The aftermath saw these people, most of whom I didn't even know, choose to describe me in derogatory ways, using words like '*mental*' and '*lunatic*.' Of course, it was all said behind my back (the worst thing when you're already paranoid.) Then for the next couple weeks people kept telling me they'd 'heard' about it. I don't have time for whispery little bitches who hunger for gossip but display no concern for your wellbeing.

All the words and stories they told were designed to warn others to stay away from me, as though I were a feral animal that would chomp off their fingers next time I snapped. All of this occurred because of a one bad stint of mental health. I can't help but wonder if people would demonstrate the same collective lack of sympathy towards someone who'd broken their leg and needed help getting up the stairs? Because both are life-interfering afflictions.

When you're charged with publicly going insane, it follows you around like a vapor trail for so long. Adjectives like 'mental' and 'crazy' become your identifying traits, used behind your back or when you try to voice how you're feeling. That's another thing society does, we brand people like cattle - and trust me, nothing stings more than being called crazy. Being called crazy is like being told to shut up. I don't mean fun crazy, I mean like 'fucking crazy.' What can you say back to that? It's so painful because in a way it disqualifies your humanity. It makes your opinion seem invalid. It's humiliating. Yet it's a word that's found a home in our everyday conversations, to such an extent it's now used to describe actions that aren't even worthy of the title.

Why do we do it? Why do we embroider words like 'crazy' onto people like scarlet letters? From personal experience, I feel there are several reasons. The first may be because culturally we enjoy watching someone float downstream. *'Oh, she's gone absolutely crazy, have you heard what she did?'* Breakdowns are often seen as an entertainment or a commodity, rather than the debilitating side-effect of a toxic health condition. The second is because, for all we talk about mental health, there's still a collective misunderstanding as to what it means.

There are often situations where people have done seemingly incomprehensible things, but we never know what is really going on in their lives. We don't know if they've been shaken by trauma; and because these traumas are private and we don't immediately have access to them, we just automatically condemn, criticise or label this person as bananas. When in reality, if we had a firmer understanding of not only mental health itself, but also the things that trigger it, we'd see that it's a direct precursor to behaviour other people claim they can't understand so just call crazy.

If we spent even a fraction of the time we dedicate to judging and directed it toward educating ourselves on all matter's mental health, we'd see a massive improvement to the lives of those around us that suffer from it. I've been victim to people calling me nuts in ways that I don't necessary think are fair, so I'd notice the possible impact if people educated themselves.

**Control.**

This essay is for anyone who has battled an eating disorder. It's about how easy it is to fall back into that mindset, especially while wrestling with poor mental health. I wrote it a while back during a particularly bad spell of depression, which was a prelude to the return of dangerous eating habits. Afterwards I revisited it and finished it with an insight I didn't have at the time.

It also discusses the crippling pressure placed on us by social media to look a certain way, and how that platforms like Instagram, Twitter and so on, perpetuates poor body image and further damages your mental health.

My periods of depression are typically characterised like so: I wake in the morning with an alarming dread, feeling a slight anger toward a world that I don't fully feel a part of. Throughout the day I tend to sob intermittently over everything and nothing. It could be a sad song, or it's triggered by empathy. Honestly the reasons range from rational to completely bonkers. I've seen me crying in my bed over a broken heart, to yelling at the washing machine as it was being too loud. Or it's the opposite side of that, and I'm an emotional iceberg. In the evenings, I either binge watch tedious Netflix shows, but don't take in a single scene; or I spend too much time with friends (also not taking anything in.) I just sort of sit there, like a Furby that's running out of batteries, occasionally chirping like a needy Tamagotchi.

Throughout the whole period I'm constantly praying for the dark cloud to lift, and my mood to pass. During this particular bad patch of mental health however, I was unprepared for how wholly it would take over my days and life.

It had been nearly two weeks and my mood continued to flip frequently, yo-yoing between wild euphoria to rabid lows. I slept less at night yet napped deeply at any given opportunity. After a while I felt as though I'd stopped participating in my own life, and all sense of control I had was relinquished to this unseen force that now dictated how my days would go.

Control. A word that haunts a lot of those who suffer from mental health issues. Control over your image, control over what others say about you, control of your life. Control over your mind. Control, the one thing I was losing grip of. Like everything insidious, it started out slowly and unseen. The return of some old control issues, nothing to worry about. Standard practice when you're feeling this low, right? For me anyway. Forty press ups at night, forty when you wake. Run a certain distance each day at the gym; got to keep that cardio up, you're beginning to look a little flabby.

"Flabby."

Nobody called me that, other than the little self-doubt troll beginning to pipe up from the back of my head.

When the obsessive thoughts about my weight reappeared, I figured that this wasn't anything to worry about. There was always a direct correlation between bad periods of mental health and my body dysmorphia. Besides, exercise is good for your mental health; because it's not just about the booty, it's also about the brain! Then the toxic thoughts started to worm their way in.

*'Let's leave half this sandwich, you don't need the full thing'* became my lunch time narrative. *'Let's start counting how many pasta shells we use, carefully sized portions.'* I mean, I didn't want to look like I had a poo belly. Whenever my stomach would groan for food, I'd pacify it with sparkling water; whenever I felt fatigued, I'd keep my energy levels up with the cans of Coke and gallons of Red Bull. The whole time I was still exercising as hard as before, only now on half the fuel.

A week later a friend idly said to me, '*you've lost weight.'* Truth be told, I'd zoned in and out of the conversation intermittently, unable to focus on anything other than how shit I felt. I sat nursing my decaf latte oblivious to the whizzing world around me, but the moment she said that it immediately caught my attention.

When I heard those words, I felt it again: that old surge of glee; that voice of accomplishment ringing in my ear. **I've. Lost. Weight.** I literally had zero control over the rest of my life or my mood, but at least I've got a handle on this.

After that I started cutting down parts of my meals. Then I started skipping them completely. Before I knew it, I'd once again submitted to the tyrannical regime that is calorie counting.              I couldn't control that my life was crumbling around me, or that no matter how hard I tried to fix it, another blow was just around the corner. This, however, I could control. I had power over what I ate – or rather, didn't eat. It wasn't even a conscious effort my mind just goes back to that as default.                    I've wrestled with eating disorders before; the most notable of them being a year-long battle with bulimia. While this was a far cry from days that saw me ramming my fingers down my throat after every meal, it was definitely not a healthy path to start back down.              I believe an eating disorder it never really goes away. Not completely. You can form strict dietary habits, execute effective gym routines; you can be told a thousand times that your body looks amazing, that you're sexy, and people can even say that they're jealous – but you never truly believe it, do you? Especially when you're going through a bad period of mental health. Whilst this was all unfolding, I posted a photo 'bragging' that I'd lost 8lbs in a week (not even three weeks prior to that photo, I'd lost nearly the same.) The reaction was a bombardment of compliments decorated with the flame emoji. All praise. *"Jealous." "Skinny as a needle!" What's your secret?"*

What's my secret? It's called the Depression Diet – and it is not good for you. Yet the praise did its part. It temporarily silenced the ghostly echoes of self-doubt. It took the edge of my depression. I felt in ownership over part of my life again. While I may not be able to control what I think of myself, I could navigate what others thought of me – and social media was the easiest way to get that. Perhaps 'easiest' was a poor choice of words. I thought a few compliments would be a remedy, but when they stopped, I only wanted to lose more weight, so I ate less and exercised more. During this period, I was so focused on my body type, that I completely ignored my mental [and physical] health. I let it take over because it was providing temporary relief from the other symptoms – but it wasn't sustainable.

Eventually I fainted at the gym.       When I was recovering, I sat on the edge of a treadmill, head between my legs. While downing a bottle of Lucozade sport and I felt utter hatred for myself. I was too embarrassed to ask someone to come get me, so eventually I pulled together enough energy to get back to the flat, where I collapsed into a heap and cried. This wasn't working. So, I later that night I ordered take out and forced myself to eat it. Okay, not the healthiest of foods, but if I was going to break this cycle, I needed to take a sledgehammer to it.

As a gay man, I am part of a society that's submissive to body image, and I as one who also suffers from poor mental health I know how easy it is to again fell prey to that toxic mindset.

Body dysmorphia mixed with depression is a deadly cocktail of self-doubt. When you're around people that are younger, prettier, skinnier, or more toned, you're setting yourself up in an environment that'll make you feel inadequate – and you can't escape that, because it's even worse online. One mindless scroll through Instagram sees you greeted with photo after photo of these tanned, toned deities; and when you're depressed, or struggling with body dysmorphia, it can be like taking a bartering ram to your self-esteem.                    I know so many gay men, like myself, that crave comments about their body. It's not attention we're seeking, but rather affirmation. This insatiable want to feel loved, hot, attractive; we want someone to tell us we're more than the heinous monster created by our low self-esteem; that the ugly mutant we see gawking back at us in the mirror is just an illusion conjured up by our depression.

Looking back now I can't help but think the reaction I got would be a sharp contrast to the one I would have received if the weight gain had been on the heavier side of the scale.

We're quick off the mark to condemn someone for being overweight, but never bother to ask why someone's losing it rapidly. Chances are it isn't a diet, but rather something else. People were happy to tell me I looked good, but never bothered to ask how I felt. We need to realise what impact these expectations can have on those who battle with eating disorders, with mental health issues, or perhaps just low self-esteem in general.          As I said earlier, any form of eating disorder and mental health issues, never truly goes away. It's always there, like a monster in a horror movie threatening to return. It's perpetuated more by a world that preaches to us the importance of having a positive body image, but then condemns you for not living up to their definition of it. It's hard living a society that's so focused on how you look but doesn't see how you feel.                    I've now regained control over both my mental health, and my eating habits. It's a slow-stepping process, but I got there. Just as you will. Just as I will in the future should either of them rear their ugly heads. Since the last battle, I've taught myself to stay off social media when I feel low; all it does is add to that sense of having no worth.

             I've also clicked that the less you eat, the worse you're going to feel. Seems like common sense, right? All I did was nap or stagger around in a zombie-like state, constantly fatigued – how is that helping my mental health?      When you're depressed you can't trust your own thoughts sometimes; when you suffer from body dysmorphia, what you see is not what others see. A lot of the time the negative comments we think others are whispering about us more often than not turn out to be ones we're saying about ourselves. Remember that. There's help out there, you just need to ask for it. The reason I shared this is because I want others to know that they are not alone.

## Why I Rarely Talk About It (In Real Life)

In the past I've had people in my life talk about being there for me as though they're performing some universally amazing act of charity. *'If you need to talk'* and other phrases rolled off their tongues without any genuine feeling. Sometimes it can feel that those remarks were offered up those out of obligation, to soothe their guilt, because if I did do something – *something permeant* – then at least they'd be able to sleep at night knowing they did the bare minimum.

Do people really care? Some of them, sure. You always spot authenticity I feel. Others however… Well, let's just say we all know those people who're so blissfully tangled upon in their life they seldom spare a moment to help you unknot yours.

How many times have you approached someone about a problem or issue that's gnawing away at your mental health only to have it met with deadening silence? Even though you've entertained their countless meltdowns and rants without hesitation. Then when it happens to you, they can't even conjure up the energy to text back. *'Oh, look, Topher is feeling sad again. Must be Tuesday.'*

When this happens to me, I immediately regret opening my mouth. After any frantic burn-out you also lose a sense of dignity as your privacy feels like a foregone conclusion.

In those moments I felt so small; I felt like a burden, like an unwanted chore. A task that must be finished rather than a person that needed saving. Even then, after seeing the psychical signs of inner trauma, some people just stopped asking *'how you are?'*
It is bad enough depression has its claws in so deep there's zero chance you can wriggle free; but when the

person you've gone to for solace treats you in an unhelpful way, it can often feel like too much.

So, what do we do? I'll tell you what I do, I shrink into myself. That's why so many of us don't talk about it because society makes it abundantly clear your cries are falling on deaf or indifferent ears. Everyone has their own issues, that is true; but as humans we should try to juggle our own struggles while also extending a supportive hand to others we love too.

Once again, I'll say the only way to solve this problem is by understanding it; by educating ourselves on it. If we spare five minutes to understand the narrative behind someone's breakdown, or 'odd' behaviour then we will be better equipped to handle any similar situations that arise in the future. But until we reach the point where we can ask with unquestionable concern *how are you*?' I don't really want to 'talk about it.'

*Thank you for taking the time to read this book – it really means a lot. Gay & Tired, volume 1 and 2, are self-published. In order for me to have a chance of getting a publishing contract I need to get my name out there more.*

*It's with that said I ask you to share your thoughts on these essays on social media, or even leave a review on Amazon.*

*Once again, thank you.*

*All the Love.*

*Topher.*

*xoxo*

Printed by Amazon Italia Logistica S.r.l.
Torrazza Piemonte (TO), Italy

10335013R00062

e all have those days where we're just a confused wee ball of anger, ready to detonate at any given moment. Anger at your boss, anger at life, anger at love, anger at your dog because *they* can't text you back.

Gay and Tired Volume 2 covers the entire circus that adulthood invites us to. It dissects my anger, my meltdowns and my most debilitating thoughts; it digs up their roots, and lays them out before you.

It *won't* help you become a better person, but it might make you feel a little less alone (or comparatively less psycho.) After all we're all just weary travellers, stumbling through the ennui and doldrums searching for something or someone to relate to.

ISBN 9781076327574

90000

Selected Fiction of
John Riddell

# Writing Surfaces

derek beaulieu and
Lori Emerson, editors